# Vanhorn Bondholders Protective Committee, Petitioner, v. Louis A. Green et al. U.S. Supreme Court Transcript of Record with Supporting Pleadings

U.S. Supreme Court, OSCAR S ROSNER, Additional Contributors

*Vanhorn Bondholders Protective Committee, Petitioner, v. Louis A. Green et al.*

Petition / U.S. Supreme Court / 1946 / 44 / 329 U.S. 833 / 67 S.Ct. 498 / 91 L.Ed. 706 / 2-15-1946
Vanhorn Bondholders Protective Committee, Petitioner, v. Louis A. Green et al.
Brief in Opposition (P) / OSCAR S ROSNER / 1946 / 44 / 329 U.S. 833 / 67 S.Ct. 498 / 91 L.Ed. 706 / 3-7-1946
Vanhorn Bondholders Protective Committee, Petitioner, v. Louis A. Green et al.
Petition for Rehearing / RICHARD B HAND / 1946 / 44 / 329 U.S. 833 / 67 S.Ct. 498 / 91 L.Ed. 706 / 1-3-1947
Vanhorn Bondholders Protective Committee, Petitioner, v. Louis A. Green et al.
Reply Brief / GEORGE W JAQUES / 1946 / 44 / 329 U.S. 833 / 67 S.Ct. 498 / 91 L.Ed. 706 / 3-21-1946
Vanhorn Bondholders Protective Committee, Petitioner, v. Louis A. Green et al.
Petitioner's Brief / RICHARD B HAND / 1946 / 44 / 329 U.S. 833 / 67 S.Ct. 498 / 91 L.Ed. 706 / 9-28-1946
Vanhorn Bondholders Protective Committee, Petitioner, v. Louis A. Green et al.
Respondent's Brief / OSCAR S ROSNER / 1946 / 44 / 329 U.S. 833 / 67 S.Ct. 498 / 91 L.Ed. 706 / 10-12-1946

Vanhorn Bondholders Protective Committee,
Petitioner, v. Louis A. Green et al. U.S. Supreme
Court Transcript of Record with Supporting
Pleadings

Table of Contents

# Supreme Court of the United States

OCTOBER TERM, 1945.

---

No.

---

IN THE MATTER

*of*

VANHORN BONDHOLDERS PROTECTIVE COMMITTEE,

*Petitioner,*

*against*

LOUIS A. GREEN and ROBERT HEILBRUNN, Known in these
Proceedings as the Green Committee and
Morris Green, *et al.,*

*Respondents.*

---

## PETITION FOR WRITS OF CERTIORARI TO THE UNITED STATES CIRCUIT COURT OF APPEALS FOR THE SIXTH CIRCUIT AND SUPPORTING BRIEF.

---

*To the Honorable the Chief Justice of the United States and the Associate Justices of the Supreme Court of the United States:*

Your Petitioner, the Vanhorn Protective Committee, for First Mortgage Bondholders of Inland, respectfully shows:

## Summary Statement of the Matter Involved.

The Circuit Court of Appeals for the Sixth Circuit ruled that overdue coupons on the First Mortgage Bonds of Inland Gas Corporation, a Debtor in proceedings under Chapter X of the Bankruptcy Act, do not bear simple interest, as provided in the Mortgage or Deed of Trust securing the Bonds, from the respective due dates of such coupons. Review of that decision is sought by another Committee, known as the Vanston Committee which has filed a petition for Writs of Certiorari with this Court (October Term, 1945, No. 248-9) at or about the same time as this is filed. In its petition, said Vanston Committee has set forth a summary statement of the matter involved. In order that repetition may be avoided, Petitioner herein respectfully adopts that statement.

## Opinions Below.

The opinion of the Circuit Court of Appeals is reported 151 Fed. (2d) at p. 470. Application was made by the Vanston Committee to the Circuit Court of Appeals for reargument which application was supported by petitioner herein. That application was denied November 26, 1945.

With its petition the Vanston Committee has presented to this Court, as an exhibit thereto, a duly certified transcript of the printed record in the case as the same appears in the United States Circuit Court of Appeals for the Sixth Circuit. Petitioner herein adopts that transcript.

## Jurisdictional Statement.

Jurisdiction to review this case upon writs of certiorari is expressly conferred upon this Court by Judicial Code, Section 240, as amended (Act of March 3, 1891, c. 517,

Sec. 6, 26 Stat. 828; Act of March 3, 1911, c. 231, Sec. 240, 36 Stat. 1157; Act of February 13, 1925, c. 229, Sec. 1, 43 Stat. 938; U. S. C. Title 28, Sec. 347).

## Questions Presented.

1. Whether in determining the rule for the choice of the governing law covering the validity of an interest provision in a multi-State contract made by a Debtor in Chapter X Bankruptcy Proceedings the Circuit Court of Appeals should select the rule of the forum State.

2. Whether such provision is invalid, although it does not violate the public policy of any of the States involved, nor of the United States, and would have been upheld if it had been litigated in the Courts of any of such States.

## Reasons Relied on for Granting the Writs

Petitioner herein adopts the reasons relied on for granting the writs as same are set forth in the above mentioned petition to this Court filed by the Vanston Committee.

## Specifications of Errors to be Urged.

Petitioner herein adopts the Specifications of Errors as set forth in the Vanston Petition.

## Prayer for Writs

Wherefore, your petitioner respectfully prays that a writ of certiorari be issued out of and under the seal of this Court to the United States Circuit Court of Appeals for the Sixth Circuit commanding said last named Court to certify and send to this Honorable Court a full and complete transcript of the record of all proceedings in the within cause and to stand to and abide by such order and direction as to your Honors shall seem meet and the circumstances of the case require and that your petitioner may have such other and further relief or remedy in the premises as to this Court may seem proper.

Dated: New York, N. Y., February 15, 1946.

ROBERT J. BULKLEY,
*Counsel for Petitioner.*

RICHARD B. HAND,
111 Broadway,
New York 6, N. Y.,
*Attorney for Petitioner.*

ROBERT J. BULKLEY,
Bulkley Building,
Cleveland 15, Ohio,
*Of Counsel.*

# 𝔖upreme 𝔠ourt of the 𝔘nited 𝔖tates

OCTOBER TERM, 1945

---

No.

---

IN THE MATTER

*of*

VANHORN BONDHOLDERS PROTECTIVE COMMITTEE,
*Petitioner,*

*against*

LOUIS A. GREEN and ROBERT HEILBRUNN, Known in these
Proceedings as the Green Committee and
Morris Green, *et al.,*
*Respondents.*

---

## BRIEF IN SUPPORT OF PETITION
## FOR WRITS OF CERTIORARI.

Petitioner herein adopts all of the argument of the
Vanston Committee as fully as if same were herein
repeated.

ROBERT J. BULKLEY,
*Of Counsel.*

# Supreme Court of the United States

## OCTOBER TERM, 1945.

### Nos. 850, 851. 44 - 45

In the Matter

of

VANHORN BONDHOLDERS PROTECTIVE COMMITTEE,

*Petitioner,*

—against—

LOUIS A. GREEN and ROBERT HEILBRUNN, Known in these proceedings as the Green Committee and MORRIS GREEN, *et al.,*

*Respondents.*

---

## BRIEF OF GREEN COMMITTEE AND MORRIS GREEN IN OPPOSITION TO PETITION FOR WRIT OF CERTIORARI.

---

OSCAR S. ROSNER,
*Counsel for Respondents,*
*Green Committee and Morris Green.*

BAKER, OBERMEIER, ROSNER & ROSENSON,
*Attorneys for Respondents,*
*Green Committee and Morris Green.*

OSCAR S. ROSNER,
JAY RAYMOND LEVINSON,
*Of Counsel.*

THE COURT PRESS, N. Y. C.

# Supreme Court of the United States

## OCTOBER TERM, 1945.

### Nos. 850, 851.

————◆————

In the Matter

of

VANHORN BONDHOLDERS PROTECTIVE COMMITTEE,
*Petitioner,*

—against—

LOUIS A. GREEN and ROBERT HEILBRUNN, Known in
these proceedings as the Green Committee and
MORRIS GREEN, *et al.,*

*Respondents.*

————◆————

## BRIEF OF GREEN COMMITTEE AND MORRIS GREEN IN OPPOSITION TO PETITION FOR WRIT OF CERTIORARI.

Since the petitioner herein adopts all of the reasons
and argument of the Vanston Committee petition
(No. 848 and No. 849), the respondents herein beg
leave to refer to their entire brief submitted in opposition to No. 848 and No. 849 as if same were herein repeated.

Respectfully submitted,

OSCAR S. ROSNER,
*Counsel for Respondents,*
*Green Committee and Morris Green.*

BAKER, OBERMEIER, ROSNER & ROSENSON,
*Attorneys for Respondents,*
*Green Committee and Morris Green.*

OSCAR S. ROSNER,
JAY RAYMOND LEVINSON,
*Of Counsel.*

IN THE

# Supreme Court of the United States

OCTOBER TERM, 1946.

## No. 44.

## No. 45.

IN THE MATTER OF

AMERICAN FUEL & POWER COMPANY, INLAND GAS CORPORA-
TION, KENTUCKY FUEL GAS CORPORATION, *Debtors.*

VAN HORN BONDHOLDERS PROTECTIVE COMMITTEE, *Petitioner,*

v.

LOUIS A. GREEN AND ROBERT HEILBRUNN, Known in these
Proceedings as the GREEN COMMITTEE AND MORRIS
GREEN, *Respondents.*

VAN HORN BONDHOLDERS PROTECTIVE COMMITTEE, *Petitioner,*

v.

CARL B. EARLY, DANIEL MATTHEWS, THOMAS MATTHEWS, JACK
PATTON AND P. G. MEADOR, *Respondents.*

## PETITION FOR REHEARING.

ROBERT J. BULKLEY,
HERBERT G. PILLEN,
Munsey Building,
Washington 11, D. C.
*Attorneys for Petitioner.*

*Of Counsel:*
RICHARD B. HAND,
111 Broadway,
New York 6, New York.

PRESS OF BYRON S. ADAMS, WASHINGTON, D. C

IN THE

# Supreme Court of the United States

OCTOBER TERM, 1946.

No. 44.

No. 45.

IN THE MATTER OF

AMERICAN FUEL & POWER COMPANY, INLAND GAS CORPORA-
TION, KENTUCKY FUEL GAS CORPORATION. *Debtors.*

VAN HORN BONDHOLDERS PROTECTIVE COMMITTEE, *Petitioner,*

v.

LOUIS A. GREEN AND ROBERT HEILBRUNN, Known in these
Proceedings as the GREEN COMMITTEE AND MORRIS
GREEN, *Respondents.*

VAN HORN BONDHOLDERS PROTECTIVE COMMITTEE, *Petitioner,*

v.

CARL B. EARLY, DANIEL MATTHEWS, THOMAS MATTHEWS, JACK
PATTON AND P. G. MEADOR, *Respondents.*

## PETITION FOR REHEARING.

A rehearing of these cases is respectfully sought by Van
Horn Bondholders Protective Committee because affirmance
of the orders of the United States Circuit Court of Appeals
for the Sixth Circuit will not accomplish the equitable distribution of assets of the bankrupt estate which is required

by the opinion of this Court, but, on the contrary, will defeat equity.

Certiorari was granted because of the importance of the questions raised, and this Court rejected the reasoning of the Circuit Court of Appeals, adopting an approach to the problem which was not suggested by counsel in brief or in oral argument, and was not considered by the District Court nor by the Circuit Court. This petitioner unreservedly accepts and adopts the principles expressed in this Court's opinion, but represents that the broad question of balancing creditors' equities was so submerged in the argument under a technical discussion of conflicts of laws, that it was not adequately presented to this Court, and a rehearing is now necessary to assure just application of the declared controlling principles to the facts of this situation.

The opinion of this Court recognized that the general rule stopping the accrual of interest at the beginning of bankruptcy proceedings is modified by equities running in favor of secured creditors under certain circumstances, and that "the touchstone of each decision on allowance of interest in bankruptcy, receivership and reorganization has been a balance of equities between creditor and creditor or between creditors and the debtor."

As against a static bankrupt estate comprising a fixed property to be distributed among creditors it may well be that, during a delay deemed necessary to the administration of the estate, interest should not accrue to a preferred creditor at the cost of depriving a junior creditor of any part of his just claim. That is not this case.

This case is the converse. Inland is not a static estate, but an active one, and has produced good profits under the administration of the Court. A prompt liquidation at the time that Inland went into receivership would probably have paid nothing to junior creditors, as there were no unmortgaged assets. But the Court undertook the operation of the bankrupt estate, and, although the whole property was under the first mortgage, withheld from the bondholders accruing earnings which might have been applied to paying bond interest. With these funds so borrowed from the bondholders, the court's trustee acquired additional property, enlarged the bankrupt's facilities and earning capacity, and prospered increasingly.

It is agreed that bondholders should not profit at the expense of junior creditors by a delay ordered by a bankruptcy court in the settlement of a static estate. But in this case of an active estate profitably administered, we seek the chance to establish the equity that profits flowing from the use of the mortgaged property should be available to pay the bondholders an honest return for the use of the property under their mortgage and on the funds withheld from them to initiate and sustain the profitable operation. In equity a static estate should not be depleted to pay interest at the cost of junior creditors, but the working profits of mortgaged property should not enrich junior creditors and stockholders at the cost of using bondholders' capital without compensation.

The first mortgage bondholders have been compelled to forego the use of money which they had a right to get by the terms of the indenture. Solely by the use of the mortgaged property and its avails the trustee has accumulated enough to pay the bondholders in full, including interest on interest as the indenture provides, and also to pay the full face amount of the second mortgage securities.[1] Is it equity to abstract from the earnings of the mortgaged estate available funds which the indenture promised to these first mortgage investors, and ultimately divert them to payment of interest on the second mortgage? And shall we so pay to the second mortgage investors principal in full plus interest in full plus interest on unpaid interest instalments,

---

[1] All the accumulations of earnings were made possible by use of mortgaged property and its avails. That such accumulations have proven sufficient to pay indebtedness to the extent stated is due to the subordination of substantial claims of Columbia Gas & Electric Company, a controversy not directly involved here.

which is provided for also in the second mortgage indenture?

If payment of interest on interest is denied to the first mortgage there will probably be enough to pay interest on interest on the second mortgage. Although that seems inequitable it might result from an affirmance of the Circuit Court of Appeals. In the alternative, if second mortgage interest on interest is denied, there may well be funds remaining for the unjust enrichment of the holding company which owns the common stock of the debtor, at the cost of both first and second mortgage security holders. Or there might be a payment on the Columbia Gas & Electric claims, which the courts have subordinated because Columbia acquired them in violation of the Federal Antitrust Laws for the purpose of stifling the threatened competition of Inland. (*Columbia Gas & Electric Corp.* v. *United States, et al.,* 151 F. (2) 461, cert. denied October 14, 1946.)

The undersigned counsel ask this rehearing with humility, conceding that the record here may be inadequate to determine all the equities among creditors. Our apology is that we brought up to this Court a record covering the issues made by our opponents on their appeal from the District Court. The record even as it is, while it may not reveal the whole equity involved, is fully adequate to show the inequity which will result from a simple affirmance of the Circuit Court of Appeals.

In these cases the District Court and the Circuit Court of Appeals both assumed that the result must depend upon the validity under the New York law of a covenant to pay interest on matured interest coupons. This Court granted certiorari to establish the rule that a distribution by a bankruptcy court should be governed by the broader equities inherent in the policy of the Bankruptcy Act. Manifestly there has been no adequate argument of the equities here involved. A reargument will enable this Court to decide whether the required "balance of equities" can be better determined by this Court on this record, or by remand for further proceedings in the District Court.

# CERTIFICATE.

We, the undersigned attorneys for the petitioner above named, certify that the foregoing petition for a rehearing is presented in good faith and not for delay.

ROBERT J. BULKLEY,
HERBERT G. PILLEN,
*Attorneys for Petitioner.*

*Of Counsel:*

RICHARD B. HAND,

January 3, 1947.

# Supreme Court of the United States

OCTOBER TERM, 1945

No. 848   42

No. 849   43

IN THE MATTER

of

AMERICAN FUEL & POWER COMPANY,
INLAND GAS CORPORATION,
KENTUCKY FUEL GAS CORPORATION,
*Debtors.*

---

VANSTON BONDHOLDERS PROTECTIVE COMMITTEE,
*Petitioner,*
*against*

LOUIS A. GREEN and ROBERT HEILBRUNN, Known in these
Proceedings as the Green Committee and Morris Green,
*Respondents.*

VANSTON BONDHOLDERS PROTECTIVE COMMITTEE,
*Petitioner,*
*against*

CARL B. EARLY, DANIEL MATTHEWS, THOMAS MATTHEWS,
JACK PATTON and P. G. MEADOR,
*Respondents.*

---

## REPLY BRIEF OF PETITIONER

---

GEORGE W. JAQUES,
*Counsel for Petitioner.*

MILBANK, TWEED, HOPE, HADLEY & McCLOY
and GEORGE W. JAQUES,
*Attorneys for Petitioner.*

GEORGE W. JAQUES,
LeWRIGHT BROWNING,
*Of Counsel.*

# TABLE OF CASES

# Supreme Court of the United States

OCTOBER TERM, 1945

---

No. 848

---

No. 849

---

IN THE MATTER

of

AMERICAN FUEL & POWER COMPANY,
INLAND GAS CORPORATION,
KENTUCKY FUEL GAS CORPORATION,

*Debtors.*

---

VANSTON BONDHOLDERS PROTECTIVE COMMITTEE,

*Petitioner,*

*against*

LOUIS A. GREEN and ROBERT HEILBRUNN, Known in these
Proceedings as the Green Committee and Morris Green,

*Respondents.*

VANSTON BONDHOLDERS PROTECTIVE COMMITTEE,

*Petitioner,*

*against*

CARL B. EARLY, DANIEL MATTHEWS, THOMAS MATTHEWS,
JACK PATTON and P. G. MEADOR,

*Respondents.*

---

## REPLY BRIEF IN SUPPORT OF PETITION FOR WRITS OF CERTIORARI

The main contention in Respondents' briefs seems to
be that no real question of choice of law is involved (Early
et al. brief p. 6; Green Committee brief pp. 3, 7). This
despite the fact that the Circuit Court of Appeals recog-

nized it could reach the question of the validity of the interest provision only after having ascertained "from what
source we should seek controlling jurisprudence" (R. 381;
151 F. (2d) p. 475; Petition, p. 3).

Analysis of the instant case is not advanced by the
attempt of respondent Green Committee to inject into the
discussion diversity cases like *Ruhlin* vs. *New York Life
Insurance Company*, 304 U. S. 202 (1937) and *Huddleston*
vs. *Dwyer*, 322 U. S. 232 (1943). We submit that diversity
cases differ from the instant bankruptcy case in that, as
was said by this Court in *Holmberg* vs. *Armbrecht et al.*,
decided February 25, 1946,

> "For purposes of diversity suits a Federal court
> is in effect 'only another court of the state' *Guaranty
> Trust Company* vs. *York, supra*, at 108."

In bankruptcy, where the jurisdiction of the Federal
court is derived from another constitutional source*, the
basic rule as to application of State law is different. See
*American Surety Company* vs. *Sampsell*, decided February
25, 1946, where this Court said:

> "True, we stated in both *Prudence* opinions that
> the federal law governing distribution of a bankrupt's
> estate should be applied with 'appropriate regard for
> rights acquired under rules of state law'. But the ex-
> tent to which state law is to be so considered is in the
> last analysis a matter of federal law."

The Early et al. brief seems to rely largely on a footnote in *Corn Exchange Bank* vs. *Klauder*, 318 U. S. 434, 437
(1942). The transaction there, however, did not have substantial contacts with more than one state, and thus did not
raise the issue of the proper source for choice of law rules

* *Duggan et al.* vs. *Sansberry*, decided by this Court March 4,
1946.

in federal bankruptcy proceedings. The transaction in the instant case, on the other hand, aside from its contacts in *New York* and *Illinois*, involves distribution of cash accumulated by the Trustee through the operation of the mortgaged properties located in *Kentucky*. Furthermore, these respondents, by their emphasis on *Klaxon Co.* vs. *Stentor Co.*, 313 U. S. 487 (1941) (brief p. 11), and by their reliance on what they consider to be the Kentucky choice of law rule (brief p. 15), admit that a serious question of choice of law stands at the threshold of the case at bar.

Both respondents argue that there is no evidence of record that any bondholder demanded payment in Illinois. Anticipating this argument, we have pointed out in a footnote on page 14 of our original brief that "during all the period when these coupons became due the Company was either in Federal Equity Receivership or in 77-B or Chapter X proceedings." It is clear that by "these coupons" we meant the coupons involved in this litigation and both respondents have to admit that all of the coupons here involved fell due while the Company was in some kind of insolvency proceedings (Green Committee brief pp. 7, 8; Early et al. brief p. 8). The last semi-annual coupon paid was that due August 1, 1930, and receivership occurred December 2, 1930 (R. 303, 173).

The coupons here involved thus remained uncollected and the holder's right to demand payment in Illinois remained unimpaired. That some earlier coupons appear to have been paid prior to any insolvency proceeding, is immaterial. The record does not show that these earlier coupons were presented in New York, and respondents' attempt, in the face of a clear contractual provision establishing an optional place of performance in Illinois (R. 354, 355, 360), to eliminate that State as one of those substantially connected with the transaction, finds no support in the record.*

Respondents (especially Early et al. brief p. 7) also argue that since New York is named ahead of Chicago in the contract, New York must be regarded as the sole place of performance for purposes of choice of law. This contention, which is asserted as "axiomatic" and based upon "the general rule", begs the principal question of the case, by simply assuming that under the applicable choice of law rule (which rule?) Illinois and Kentucky are not regarded as substantially connected with the transaction. Thus respondents are merely contending for a particular choice of law rule, while Petitioner is contending for another.

This choice of law question, since it arises in bankruptcy, should be controlled by the federal choice of law rule which was laid down in *Seeman* vs. *Philadelphia Warehouse Company*, 274 U. S. 403 (1927). Respondents seek to eliminate the latter case by pointing out that it was decided prior to *Erie* vs. *Tompkins*, 304 U. S. 64 (1938). Here again they beg the question. The *Seeman* case, which is a choice of law case (as distinguished from the purely local situation in *Corn Exchange Bank* vs. *Klauder, supra*) is still the law unless overruled by the choice of law case of *Klaxon Co.* vs. *Stentor Co.*, 313 U. S. 487 (1941), and

---

* Since it was the promisee's option to select the place of performance, Illinois or New York, we fail to see how Section 356 of the *Restatement of the Law of Conflict of Laws* aids respondents. The applicable part of that section reads as follows:

"(1) When a contract involves a promise to do one thing or another at the option of either party the place of performance is undetermined *until the option is exercised,* and it *then* becomes the place of performing the promise which is chosen by the party having the option." (Italics ours.)

whether the *Klaxon* case is applicable in bankruptcy is the very question presented by the instant case.

To our collection of lower court decisions showing confusion as to the source from which the applicable choice of law rule should be drawn in bankruptcy proceedings, there should be added a recent case from the Ninth Circuit, *Hamaker* vs. *Heffron*, 148 F. (2d) 981, 983, footnote 3 (C. C. A. 9, 1945), where the court, in determining the applicable choice of law rule, was guided by federal authorities. The Ninth Circuit and the Sixth Circuit are thus on opposite sides of the fence, whereas the Eighth Circuit seems to have wavered between the two positions.

Respectfully submitted,

GEORGE W. JAQUES,
*Counsel for Petitioner.*

MILBANK, TWEED, HOPE, HADLEY & McCLOY
and GEORGE W. JAQUES,
*Attorneys for Petitioner.*

GEORGE W. JAQUES,
LEWRIGHT BROWNING,
*Of Counsel.*

# In the Supreme Court of the United States

OCTOBER TERM, 1946.

## No. 44.
## No. 45.

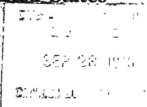

In the Matter of

AMERICAN FUEL & POWER COMPANY, INLAND GAS
CORPORATION, KENTUCKY FUEL GAS CORPORATION,

*Debtors.*

VAN HORN BONDHOLDERS PROTECTIVE COMMITTEE,

*Petitioner,*

*against*

LOUIS A. GREEN AND ROBERT HEILBRUNN,
Known in these Proceedings as the
GREEN COMMITTEE AND MORRIS GREEN,

*Respondents.*

VAN HORN BONDHOLDERS PROTECTIVE COMMITTEE,

*Petitioner,*

*against*

CARL B. EARLY, DANIEL MATTHEWS, THOMAS
MATTHEWS, JACK PATTON AND P. G. MEADOR,

*Respondents.*

## BRIEF FOR PETITIONER.

ROBERT J. BULKLEY,
Bulkley Building,
Cleveland 15, Ohio,
*Counsel for Petitioner.*

RICHARD B. HAND,
111 Broadway,
New York 6, New York,
*Attorney for Petitioner.*

THE GATES LEGAL PUBLISHING CO., CLEVELAND, OHIO—MAIN 5547

# INDEX.

## TABLE OF AUTHORITIES.

### Cases.

### Statutes.

# In the Supreme Court of the United States

OCTOBER TERM, 1946.

## No. 44.
## No. 45.

IN THE MATTER OF

AMERICAN FUEL & POWER COMPANY, INLAND GAS
CORPORATION, KENTUCKY FUEL GAS CORPORATION,

*Debtors.*

VAN HORN BONDHOLDERS PROTECTIVE COMMITTEE,

*Petitioner,*

*against*

LOUIS A. GREEN AND ROBERT HEILBRUNN,
Known in these Proceedings as the
GREEN COMMITTEE AND MORRIS GREEN,

*Respondents.*

VAN HORN BONDHOLDERS PROTECTIVE COMMITTEE,

*Petitioner,*

*against*

CARL B. EARLY, DANIEL MATTHEWS, THOMAS
MATTHEWS, JACK PATTON AND P. G. MEADOR,

*Respondents.*

## BRIEF FOR PETITIONER.

### OPINIONS OF COURTS BELOW.

The District Court rendered no opinion but during argument stated the grounds for its decision (R. 56), and thereafter made an order and judgment embodying findings of fact and conclusions of law (R. 192).

The opinion of the Circuit Court of Appeals, Sixth Circuit, is reported 151 F. (2d) 470 (1945), and is also reprinted at R. 214 *et seq.*

## JURISDICTION.

The judgments of the Circuit Court of Appeals which Petitioner seeks to have reviewed were filed on October 9, 1945 (R. 213, 214). A timely petition for re-hearing was made to the Circuit Court of Appeals (R. 234, 235) and was denied November 26, 1945 (R. 241). The petition for writs of certiorari made on behalf of Van Horn Bondholders Protective Committee was filed herein on February 15, 1946. The order of this Court granting the writs of certiorari was filed March 25, 1946 (R. 242).

Jurisdiction to review this case upon writs of certiorari is expressly conferred upon this Court by Judicial Code, Section 240, as amended (Act of March 3, 1891, c. 517, Sec. 6, 26 Stat. 828; Act of March 3, 1911, c. 231, Sec. 240, 36 Stat. 1157; Act of February 13, 1925, c. 229, Sec. 1, 43 Stat. 938; 28 U. S. C., Sec. 347), and by Bankruptcy Act, Sec. 24(c), as amended (Act of June 22, 1938, c. 575, Sec. 1, 52 Stat. 854; 11 U. S. C., Sec. 47).

## STATEMENT OF CASE.

The Circuit Court of Appeals, in a proceeding under Chapter X of the Bankruptcy Act, invalidated an express agreement that overdue bond coupons should bear simple interest from their respective due dates, which agreement had been sustained by the District Court.

The "Statement of Case" as presented in the brief filed by the Vanston Committee in the companion cases, Nos. 42 and 43, is adequate and need not be here repeated. We adopt it as our own statement.

## QUESTIONS PRESENTED.

1. Whether in determining the rule for the choice of the governing local law concerning the validity of an interest provision in a multi-State contract made by a Debtor in Chapter X Proceedings the bankruptcy court should select the choice of law rule of the forum State.

2. Whether a corporate undertaking to pay simple interest on overdue bond coupons is invalid, although it does not violate the public policy of any of the States involved, nor of the United States, and would have been upheld if it had been litigated in the Courts of any of such States.

## SUMMARY OF ARGUMENT.

1. Question No. 1 is argued by the Vanston Committee in the companion cases, Nos. 42 and 43, and that argument is adopted by petitioners herein.

2. The Indenture provision for the payment of interest on overdue coupons which was struck down by the Circuit Court of Appeals does not violate the public policy of the United States nor of any of the States involved.

## ARGUMENT.

Petitioners herein are in agreement with the argument made on behalf of the Vanston Committee in the companion cases, Nos. 42 and 43. This brief is confined to a further discussion of the public policy of the State of New York with reference to the problem herein presented.

### The covenant to pay interest on overdue interest coupons is not contrary to the public policy of New York.

The public policy of the State of New York with respect to agreements providing for the payment of interest on debt has been clearly indicated by the action of the New York Legislature, in the enactment of the usury laws. The laws of New York expressly declare that any agreement to pay interest at a rate in excess of 6% per annum is usurious and void. (N. Y. General Business Law Secs. 370, 371, 372, 373.) Although it has long been held that any such agreement, whether voluntarily made or somehow exacted, violates this Statute and will not be enforced, yet corporations are *expressly excluded* from the protection of this law (N. Y. General Business Law Sec. 374) and the Courts of New York have enforced corporate agreements to pay interest in excess of 6%. (*Union Estates Company v. Adlon Construction Co.,* 221 N. Y. 183, where an interest rate of 23% was sustained.)

Where the Circuit Court fell into error was through interpreting New York decisions which protected an individual from oppressive interest as reflecting the public policy of New York on *all* interest questions, even those involving a *corporate* borrower. No citation of authority from the New York Court of Appeals—or from the New York Appellate Division—is given to support this view, and we do not believe that any can be found.

The case of *Young v. Hill,* 67 N. Y. 162, is cited as the leading case in New York on the question of validity of agreements to pay interest on interest. That case was one between individuals, and the reasons of public policy which justified the court in ruling that compound interest would not be enforced are clearly stated in the opinion, which also made clear that, notwithstanding the rule, there still may be enforcible obligations to pay interest on interest arising even from implied agreements, when such agreements are essentially fair.

The learned judges who participated in the case of *Young v. Hill* in 1876 would be surprised to learn that, seventy years later, the salutary rule of that case would be invoked to justify the repudiation by a *corporation* of an undertaking voluntarily made by it in favor of hundreds of innocent investors, and their surprise would be still greater if they could know that the undertaking in question was not an agreement to pay compound interest, which produced the fantastically oppressive charge which they refused to enforce, but merely "an agreement to pay simple interest upon the several installments of interest as they became due" which the court, even in the case of the individual debtor in 1876, pointed out "might not be unreasonable or inequitable."

The rule of *Young v. Hill* was plainly intended to protect the "weak and ignorant" against extortion, not the corporation against its own voluntary promise. It is certainly not a precedent for the ruling of the Circuit Court in this case.

We have been unable to find any reported case in the New York Courts which decides the question here at issue. In the absence of precedents in the New York Courts, the Federal Courts are not without power to determine the public policy of that State. In undertaking such determination in the case at bar the Circuit Court considered, but refused to follow, the decision of Judge Patterson in *American Brake Shoe & Foundry Co. v. Interborough R. T. Co.*, 26 Fed. Supp. 954, and the dictum of Judge Clancy in *Transbel Investment Co. v. Roth*, 36 Fed. Supp. 396.

However, the question of the public policy involved in the allowance of simple interest on past due interest accrued on corporation bonds has again been presented to a Federal Court in New York since the Circuit Court's decision in the instant case. In a bankruptcy proceeding, *In Re Realty Associates Securities Corporation*, 66 Fed. Supp. 416, the United States District Court for the Eastern District of New York, on June 11, 1946, allowed to bondholders simple interest at 6% on accrued interest which remained unpaid at the maturity of the bonds, even though the debtor corporation had made no promise to pay it. At page 421, Judge Moskowitz said:

"The distinction was inferred to in *American Brake Shoe & Foundry Co. v. Interborough R. T. Co.*, D. C. S. D. N. Y., 1939, 26 F. Supp. 954, where the court stated at page 955 of 26 F. Supp.: 'Compounding interest in the adding of accumulated interest to the principal at periodic intervals. An agreement to pay simple interest on an overdue installment of interest is different. Computations show it to be far less onerous on the debtor.' The same distinction is recognized in the case which has been most often cited as authority against the validity of compound interest, *Young v. Hill*, 67 N. Y. 162, 23 Am. Rep. 99, where at page 174 of 67 N. Y., the court stated: 'An agreement to pay simple interest upon the several instalments of interest as they became due * * * might not be unreasonable or inequitable.' It is thus clear that the reason for the judicial outlawing of compound interest is based upon its being unduly oppressive and even ruinous to debtors, a criticism which does not lie against simple interest. The bondholders' claim in the instant case is only for simple interest upon a debt which has become due and is therefore not contrary to public policy.''

Coming as it does shortly after the Sixth Circuit Court had declared that the public policy of the State of New York requires repudiation of a voluntary corporate undertaking to pay simple interest on overdue coupons, this decision by a New York judge is a significant reassertion of the true public policy in New York, completely in harmony with the declared policy of the Legislature to protect individuals against oppressive interest payments while requiring corporations to pay what they promise, even by implication.

### CONCLUSION.

The judgments of the Circuit Court of Appeals, insofar as they reverse the judgment of the District Court, should be reversed with costs, and the judgment of the District Court should be affirmed with respect to the allowance of interest upon the interest coupons of the First Mortgage Bonds.

ROBERT J. BULKLEY,
*Counsel for Petitioner.*

RICHARD B. HAND,
*Attorney for Petitioner.*

# Supreme Court of the United States

## OCTOBER TERM, 1946.
## Nos. 44, 45.

In the Matter

of

AMERICAN FUEL & POWER COMPANY,
INLAND GAS CORPORATION,
KENTUCKY FUEL GAS CORPORATION,
*Debtors.*

---

VAN HORN BONDHOLDERS PROTECTIVE COMMITTEE,
*Petitioner,*

—against—

LOUIS A. GREEN and ROBERT HEILBRUNN, Known in these
Proceedings as the GREEN COMMITTEE and MORRIS GREEN,
*Respondents.*

---

VAN HORN BONDHOLDERS PROTECTIVE COMMITTEE,
*Petitioner,*

—against—

CARL B. EARLY, DANIEL MATTHEWS, THOMAS MATTHEWS,
JACK PATTON and P. G. MEADOR,
*Respondents.*

---

# BRIEF FOR RESPONDENTS
# GREEN COMMITTEE AND MORRIS GREEN.

OSCAR S. ROSNER,
*Counsel for Respondents,*
*Green Committee and Morris Green.*

BAKER, OBERMEIER, ROSNER & ROSENSON,
*Attorneys for Respondents,*
*Green Committee and Morris Green.*

OSCAR S. ROSNER,
*Of Counsel.*

JAY RAYMOND LEVINSON,
*On the Brief.*

---

THE COURT PRESS, N. Y. C.

# Supreme Court of the United States
## OCTOBER TERM, 1946.
### Nos. 44, 45.

In the Matter

of

AMERICAN FUEL & POWER COMPANY,
INLAND GAS CORPORATION,
KENTUCKY FUEL GAS CORPORATION,
*Debtors.*

---

VAN HORN BONDHOLDERS PROTECTIVE COMMITTEE,
*Petitioner,*

—against—

LOUIS A. GREEN and ROBERT HEILBRUNN, Known in these
Proceedings as the GREEN COMMITTEE and MORRIS GREEN,
*Respondents.*

---

VAN HORN BONDHOLDERS PROTECTIVE COMMITTEE,
*Petitioner,*

—against—

CARL B. EARLY, DANIEL MATTHEWS, THOMAS MATTHEWS,
JACK PATTON and P. G. MEADOR,
*Respondents.*

---

## BRIEF FOR RESPONDENTS
## GREEN COMMITTEE AND MORRIS GREEN.

The Respondents herein beg leave to refer to their
brief in the companion case, Nos. 42 and 43, and respect-

fully request the Court to consider such brief as directed also to the instant case.

Respectfully submitted,

OSCAR S. ROSNER,
*Counsel for Respondents,*
*Green Committee and Morris Green.*

BAKER, OBERMEIER, ROSNER & ROSENSON,
*Attorneys for Respondents,*
*Green Committee and Morris Green.*

OSCAR S. ROSNER,
*Of Counsel.*

JAY RAYMOND LEVINSON.
*On the Brief.*

CPSIA information can be obtained
at www.ICGtesting.com
Printed in the USA
LVOW02s0404010817

543262LV00016B/818/P